I0795732

CASA WABI

CASA WABI

*Tadao Ando, Gloria Cabral and Solano Benítez,
Damián Comas for Jorge Ambrosi and Gabriela Etchegaray, Dakin Hart, Alex Iida,
Alberto Kalach, Kengo Kuma, Alfonso Quiñones, Bernardo Quinzaños,
Alberto Ríos de la Rosa, OMA/Shohei Shigematsu, Álvaro Siza, Bosco Sodi,
Carla Sodi Ambrosi, Martino Stierli, and Rebeca Murrieta Valladares*

Rizzoli Electa

An extraordinary power of teamwork has gone into the project's success, and thanks to everyone involved—the architects, bricklayers, carpenters, palaperos, plumbers, artists, and communities as well as my studio team and galleries and all the people who have supported us. I am especially grateful to my dad, and to Lucía, Bosco, Mariana, Álvaro, comrades in a thousand battles. Gratitude goes to my cousin, Luis Urrutia, for his support, my sister Carla for shepherding the foundation, and to my mom. I thank each and every one of those involved—you are integral to this project.

—Bosco Sodi

Introduction

Martino Stierli, The Philip Johnson Chief Curator of Architecture and Design, The Museum of Modern Art, New York

Driving through the lush vegetation along the coastal highway that connects Puerto Escondido with Acapulco some 250 miles further west, nothing quite prepares you for Casa Wabi. Situated about forty minutes outside town limits at the end of a dirt road, the drama of this remarkable place reveals itself suddenly in the form of a sublime—and at nearly one thousand feet, sublimely long—wall, and a giant thatched roof, which shelters an equally enormous, airy, open space facing toward the Pacific Ocean.

The roar of the ocean's powerful waves is clearly audible and contributes to the unique acoustic experience of this magical place. Arriving at Casa Wabi feels like leaving the world behind and entering into a quasi-sacred space of contemplation and exposure to the natural elements. Its creator, the Japanese architect Tadao Ando, is rightly famous for his ability to conceive such spaces. It is based on his mastery of concrete, his attentiveness to the treatment of natural light, and his embrace of the natural surroundings as part of the design. At Casa Wabi, these elements are synthesized into the home of an artist's residency program that allows artists from all over the world to productively immerse themselves. For a visitor, Casa Wabi is an invitation to deaccelerate, to observe the passing of time, and to feel the cooling winds from the sea and the mountains on the skin.

The long concrete wall is the defining element of Ando's design. Laid out parallel to the shoreline, it divides the property into two distinct precincts—that of the sea toward the front, and that of the mountains toward the back. It is this simple yet compelling idea that produces a sense of place. All the other elements of the design, including the central meeting space, the guest cabins that house the visiting artists, the artist's studios, a gallery, a projection space, an observatory in which to watch the passing clouds in the sky, and offices, are situated strategically on both sides along this wall, which thus serves as the architectural backbone of the compound. As such, the wall is a strong gesture of disjunction.

As Ando has himself reflected with regard to one of his earlier projects, walls "at times . . . manifest a power that border on the violent. They have the power to divide space, transfigure space, and create new domains."[1] For this reason walls have historically had negative associations for many people. Ando, however, has devoted much of his thinking to interpreting this most basic element of architecture in ways that are enriching rather than menacing, inviting rather than rejecting, and liberating as much as enclosing. Indeed, the wall at Casa Wabi is not merely an impressive static object, but an agent of mobility that invites the visitor to explore and absorb the surrounding landscape, which is framed and given (aesthetic) meaning by the presence of the wall in the first place. (Only during my own promenade into this landscape am I told by my hosts that the vegetation around the building is by no means a natural setting, but rather the ingenious design of the Mexican architect Alberto Kalach, who has transformed the beachside property into a tropical garden of astonishing variety. Further back on the property, I am led to additional buildings by contemporary luminaries: among other things, an outdoor pottery studio by Álvaro Siza and a henhouse by Kengo Kuma.)

Nor is the wall simply a marker of separation; instead it is punctuated by apertures and openings relating the two precincts on either side of it visually and spatially. The wall is thus as much a divider as an intermediary in this dialectical encounter between the natural elements on either side.

The shine of the concrete wall's surface serves as a reflector for the natural light and the ever-changing moods of color of the natural surroundings. The polychromic glow is particularly intense during dusk and dawn. The wall is a device that enables and enhances the visual perception and experience of the space.
In this sense, it becomes a giant extension of the body. This dimension relies on Ando's masterful ability to create smooth, mirror-like surfaces on his bare concrete walls, an effect achieved by varnishing the formwork before the concrete is poured. (That this kind of finish is even possible in this remote part of the world is miraculous and indicative of the unconditional commitment of Ando's client Bosco Sodi and his Casa Wabi Foundation to this project). It is also this effect that metamorphoses the material substance of the wall into an immaterial and transcending experience. Ando has reflected upon concrete's inherent dematerializing qualities: "It seems to me that, at present, concrete is the most suitable material for realizing spaces created by rays of light. But the concrete I employ does not have plastic rigidity or weight. Instead, it must be homogeneous and light and must create surfaces. When they agree with my aesthetic image, walls become abstract, are negated, and approach the ultimate limit of space. Their actuality is lost, and only the space they enclose gives a sense of really existing."[2]

The other conspicuous element of Ando's design is the large communal space in the center of the compound. Its open structure and the thatched roof made of dried palm leaves (whose woven pattern produces a beautiful ornament) is a contemporary interpretation at large scale of the traditional *palapa* structure ubiquitous in the vernacular architecture of the region, here combined with Japanese precision and attention to detail.
Like its everyday cousin, this particular palapa works as a natural ventilation and cooling device in that it channels the natural winds through strategic openings at both ends of the apex. It is in this large, open space, which serves both as a gathering place for the guests of the foundation and as a platform for viewing the ocean, that the spirit of Casa Wabi is perhaps most fully embodied.
Its ethos is based as much on providing an opportunity for artists to retreat temporarily from their everyday lives as on the expectation that the artists interact with the local communities. Casa Wabi seeks to be more than a neo-colonial implant of the global art world onto a relatively disadvantaged (economically speaking) part of the world, but rather a place of long-term social engagement and dialogue between these two worlds. The communal space of the palapa is a symbolic representation of this spirit.

A Letter from Tadao Ando

February 1, 2024

Hearing Casa Wabi is already ten years old is a surprising and pleasant reminder.

I am joyful to know many artists, architects, and children have visited the site at Puerto Escondido. I can scarcely doubt the profound experience they must have had. Immersed in the magnificent scenery of the coastline with the cactus plain at their backs, they have devoted themselves to art.

Human experience is most precious when we bring a new life into the world of tomorrow. Casa Wabi is one such attempt to lead a life into the future through creativity and art.

I am truly proud to have been able to participate as an architect in this one-of-a-kind cultural project. I look forward to the continuous evolution of Casa Wabi in the next ten years, and beyond.

Entrance and Main Palapa

El Muro: Life at Casa Wabi

Carla Sodi Ambrosi, General Director, Casa Wabi Foundation

Tadao Ando designed Casa Wabi's main palapa with the idea of magnificence. One of the largest palapas in the world, the entrance to Casa Wabi greets residents and visitors with the immediate feeling of grandeur, which we believe inspires them to produce works of similar greatness.

Although Tadao Ando is Japanese, we convinced him to use a traditional Oaxacan palapa palm thatch, which protects against rain, lowers the interior temperature, and acts as an organic roof. Oaxacan palapa roofs slope steeply to help rain drain efficiently, necessary in a tropical climate with summer downpours. However, Ando preferred the slighter slope of similar Japanese thatched roofs, which are considered to be more graceful. We compromised with an intermediate slope that fulfilled the architect's vision for the space.

Casa Wabi's main palapa is the heart of our social activity. The 2,000-square-foot space sits at the perpendicular axis of the entrance road and the 1,024-foot-long wall, affectionately called "el muro," that forms the axis of the compound. Residents cross it several times a day, going to the gallery or to meditation areas. They gather at the main palapa for breakfast, lunch, and dinner, communal meals that give the residents the chance to share ideas. The 36-foot wooden dining table contributes to the intimacy and breadth of these conversations.

The main palapa is the point of departure for visitors who come to enjoy the day with us, and also serves as our great hall for formal receptions, banquets, or conferences. The beach and the pool are always visible through the open, south-facing front.

The walls everywhere are formed of concrete buffed smooth like marble. They are cool to the touch, and within the doubled walls one feels safe, protected, and free. We move along Casa Wabi's "axis," which anchors you within the vast property, or stop to contemplate the sea to the south, and the mountains to the north, through the openings or on the walkways radiating out from the wall. Casa Wabi's architecture is integral to everyone's daily experience.

P. 25: The gatehouse and main road at Casa Wabi's entrance.
P. 26, L: Overview of road south from gatehouse to compound.
P. 26, R: Newly constructed main palapa roof glimpsed from road.
P. 27: Northern entrance to main palapa with partial eastern wall.
P. 28: Detail of Tadao Ando's concrete walls and a succulent plant.
P. 29: Ornamental tree outside the shuttered northern windows.
Pp. 30–31: Northern view from south side of main palapa.
P. 32, L: Detail of supports for palapa roof.
P. 32, R: Example of sharp shadows cast by the walls and palapa.
P. 33: Afternoon light in the main palapa.
Pp. 34–35: Bosco Sodi's family quarters flank the main hall.
P. 36: Minimal leather chairs.
Pp. 36–37: Sunset reflected in the eastern hallway.
P. 37: Indoor potted cacti.
Pp. 38–39: Sunken lounge and communal dining area.
P. 40: Approaching the main palapa from the east after a storm.

Sea and Pools

Some Convictions Regarding Art, Architecture, and Oaxaca

Bosco Sodi, Founder, Casa Wabi Foundation

I am convinced that any artistic manifestation can influence and positively change a person, a group, or a society as a whole. For me, art is a food of the spirit that nourishes the whole human being. In artistic expression, the relationship established between the subject and the object is such that both the subject that creates and the object created are affected dialectically, and in this relationship, they mutually modify each other.

Although I have been living outside Mexico for more than twenty years, I am and I feel Mexican. I believe I have a responsibility to give back to my country a little of what it has given me, which has indeed been profound. It was out of this sense of patrimony that I first conceived of Casa Wabi, a foundation for artists and for Oaxaca, to which I feel a close connection both personally and artistically: my paternal grandfather traces his roots to Oaxaca, and since childhood, I have spent many memorable moments in

Puerto Escondido. Oaxaca is also a place where I have created a significant part of my work and where my children vacation under my parental eye. For these and other reasons, Casa Wabi was built on the coast of Oaxaca and emerged as a space that would celebrate art and the surrounding communities by fostering a relationship between the two. One of the greatest satisfactions of the project has been seeing the community take ownership of the space as a cultural activity center, especially vital for children and youth.

Casa Wabi is intended to be in continuous movement, much like life itself. I have always been fascinated by architecture's impact on people—the shaping of spaces and how they, in turn, affect the mood of those who occupy them. I knew Casa Wabi should be a tribute to the architecture with which I felt most connected, but I also wanted all of its architectural interventions to have a specific use and purpose for the foundation.

I have long admired Tadao Ando's work—the simplicity and personality of the concrete he uses, his handling of light, and the character his buildings develop over time. We are both interested in the *wabi-sabi* aesthetic, which derives from Buddhist teachings on transience and imperfection. Although the backbone of Casa Wabi is Tadao Ando's work, I also wanted the space to showcase other architects whose brilliant simplicity is now visible in their pavilions. Of special note is Álvaro Siza's clay pavilion, whose swooping walls are made from local bricks. Mexican architect Alberto Kalach took on the challenge of designing the project's stunning landscape and the imposing brick chimney. Jorge Ambrosi and Gabriela Etchegaray created a pavilion dedicated to conserving our endangered guayacan trees. Kengo Kuma's chicken coop exemplifies Casa Wabi's naturalistic values, while Gloria Cabral and Solano Benítez's compost pavilion celebrates humble materials. Bernardo Quinzaños's stunning Orchid Pavilion and OMA's Mushroom Pavilion further enhance the site. Casa Wabi has become a global reference point for architects, embraced by contributors, visitors, and supporters dedicated to the timeless goal of leaving a better planet for future generations.

P. 41: Wabi-sabi *details: drying rack, shutters, and driftwood.*
Pp. 42–47: Views of sea, pools, and concrete sun shelter.
P. 48: Overview of residency housing (south) and studios (north).

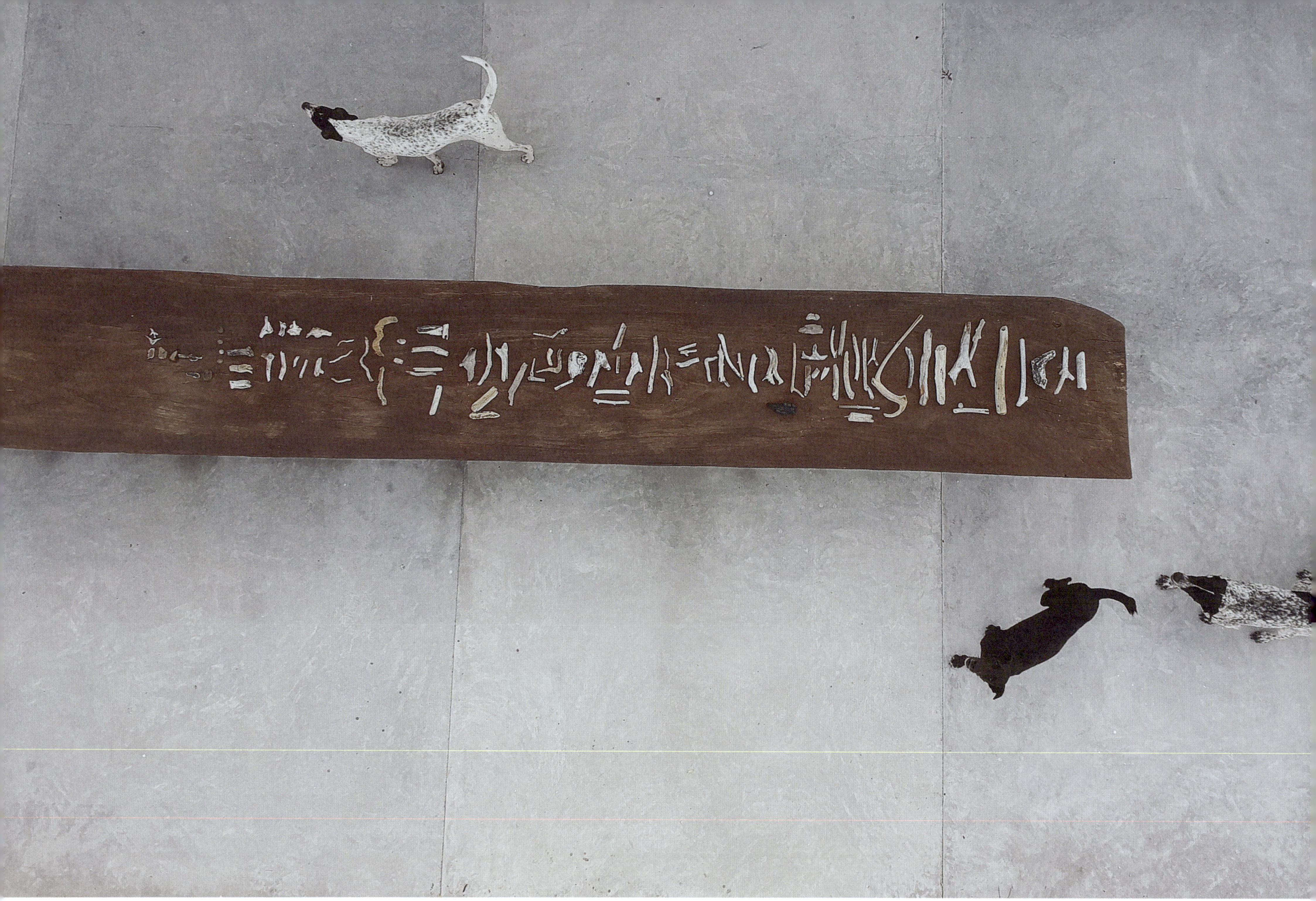

Gallery

International Art in Oaxaca

Alberto Ríos de la Rosa, Former Curator, Casa Wabi Foundation

Casa Wabi's gallery space offers exposure to acclaimed artists. The goal of the exhibitions program is to share these artists' experience within the foundation's architecture and the region's unique everyday life. For our first exhibitions, we worked with three artists who established the conceptual art movement in Europe: Daniel Buren, Michel François, and Jannis Kounellis. Buren's geometric compositions, use of primary colors, and signature three-and-a-half-inch stripes together questioned the way we perceive and use a space. The critical connection between painting and architecture was made especially visible in the conversation between the Buren work and Ando's concrete. For the second exhibition, *Tierra Vaga (Lazy Land)* by Michel François in collaboration with Harold Ancart, François created a vast and poetic diorama of Oaxaca's Costa Chica for the gallery. Simultaneously, Ancart built a large landscape mural that graphically accentuated the roughness of the natural landscape and its relationship to local popular culture. The last show in this cycle, *Jannis Kounellis*, explored memory's relationship to the human condition. Four installations represented modern elegies to labor unions, the national railroad, and historical events in Mexico.

The second cycle of exhibitions demonstrates the use of symbols from nature, as seen in the work of Ugo Rondinone, Izumi Kato, and Lawrence Weiner. These artists approach symbols in relationship to local traditions. Rondinone's sun symbolizes life, light, and strength in a show that features two moments: a suspended structure that contains more than five hundred drawings of suns made by local children, and a wool textile that reproduces one of the children's landscape drawings. Izumi Kato's aesthetic falls between the ethnographic and the oneiric, with references to surrealism, Japanese Shinto, and even African tribal art. *South of the Border* by Lawrence Weiner expresses openness to others and a rejection of nativism in all its forms. Weiner transmutes the threat of malignant geography into a one-planet dance.

The third cycle of exhibitions focuses on materials rooted in the region, particularly clay and discarded objects. Huma Bhabha's corporeal fragments create a sense of topography and interrelated parts, with the concrete bases drawing out the sculptures' terracotta hues and contrasting solidity with fragility. Claudia Comte simplifies forms found in nature, combining materials from the Oaxacan coast with meticulous methods from her studies in Switzerland. José Dávila uses construction-site refuse and the concept of collective memory to honor the past and inhabit history.

P. 57: Eastern view from gallery toward open platform.
P. 58: Southern view of open platform and grand stairs.
P. 59: Detail, Tierra Vaga, *Michel François and Harold Ancart.*
P. 60: Ugo Rondinone's installation of children's sun drawings.
P. 61: Jannis Kounellis theater doors installed in the main gallery.
Pp. 62–63: Site-specific installation by Daniel Buren.
P. 64: Izumi Kato wall hangings and sculptures.
P. 65: Detail, South of the Border, *Lawrence Weiner.*
P. 66: Nicolas Bourriaud curated residency artists in Memory Shop.
P. 67: Claudia Comte's land art ecosystem, From Where We Rise.
Pp. 68–69: Installation and detail, Touching Earth, *Huma Bhabha.*
Pp. 70–71: El Pasado Nunca es el Mismo, *José Dávila.*
P. 72: View toward open platform and stairs east from main palapa.

EN ALGÙN LUGAR AL SUR DE LA FRONTERA
SOMEWHERE SOUTH OF THE BORDER
GIRADO EN EL SENTIDO OPUE
TURNED COUNTERCLOCKWISE

TOTEM

Studio and Observatory

Integration with Nature

Bosco Sodi, Founder, Casa Wabi Foundation

When Tadao Ando and I talked about my plans for Casa Wabi's main studio, I explained that I wanted to consider the particular geography and location of the space, which is unlike my other studios. I wanted an open space, without doors or windows—where light and air would pass through all sides, where one could feel the landscape even while standing inside, where one could hear the sound of the waves, the rain, the wind. I wanted one to feel the freedom, the vegetation, the mystery of the landscape.

I wanted a place of grand dimensions that would at the same time feel cozy. The atmosphere of each studio influences one's work differently, and I'm convinced that if I did not have this studio at Casa Wabi, I wouldn't be working with clay. I cherish going to work early in the morning, when the air is fresh and the light very dim. It has become a very special place for me.

P. 73: Western view from Bosco Sodi's studio toward main palapa.
P. 74, L: A six-foot cube of smoked clay installed on the beach.
P. 74, R: Smoothing clay by hand.
P. 75: Overhead view of Bosco Sodi's studio and the observatory.
P. 76: Smoked clay cubes and spheres with wooden bench.
P. 77: Exposed beams and a sunken floor exaggerate vertical space.
P. 78: Open southern exposure toward beach.
P. 79: Studio courtyard with brick sculptures.
P. 80: Southern view of studio and observatory.
P. 81: Wooden bench for contemplating the sky.
Pp. 82–83: Cloud watching in the observatory.
P. 84: Residents use the observatory for community projects.

The Atlantes Pavilion

About Clay

Bosco Sodi, Founder, Casa Wabi Foundation

The Atlantes pavilion consists of eight rows of eight cubes each, for a total of sixty-four cubes. Each cube is six and a half feet square, which gives the sensation of the cubes holding up the sky. The cubes will change and deteriorate over time with exposure to the elements—a kind of contemporary ruin that surpasses human scale. I also wanted to make this pavilion a tribute to mud, one of the earth's elemental materials.

Modest and simple, this substance has accompanied man since time immemorial, since the day clay took away man's animal quality through plastic creation, inviting him to be human instead. Could this material be the beginning of representation? Clay is present in utensils, in ancient offerings, in the origins of all cultures—Mexico in particular.

The clay holds a great store of accumulated energy that demands the four elements carry its process to completion: the earth, from which clay is made; the water, which allows its molding and the search for form; the air to dry it; and the fire to burn and bake it.

Clay is as primal and essential as the history of man. Organic and unpredictable. It reminds me of what is actually essential, of our human essence—ruthless capitalism, fierce consumerism, technological mastery, the rush and search for the immediate, the perfection of serial production, the surface of things—these did not always exist as the project of civilization. I start from something as abstract as raw clay to achieve forms such as spheres, cubes, or cuboids. I do everything with my own hands touching the mud. I don't use molds. And soon I arrive at these human forms: imperfect and unique.

Later, I leave the pieces to dry in the shade, in the open. Then, little by little the wind caresses them and cures them. From there, I move the bricks to dry in the sun: the continuous heat removes all moisture and gives way to the hardness of stone. Finally, I smoke them in a rustic oven, using different materials, like the hulls of coconuts, for different periods of time to create unrepeatable results. I enjoy the unpredictability of the process and the grand finale when the brick is revealed, unique in its colors and textures. The defects, the cracks—as in my paintings—are a species of resistance, a reminder of the essence of man, the impermanence of things, the force of nature, and, in the end, a tribute to man and to the essential.

P. 85: Bosco Sodi shapes clay by hand before curing and smoking it.
Pp. 86–87: Kilns smoking clay with coconut husks from dawn to dusk.
P. 88: Finished bricks prepared for installation.
P. 89: Overview of Atlantes pavilion.
P. 90: Southern view of Atlantes pavilion at dusk.
P. 91: Each cube of Atlantes *is six and a half feet tall.*
P. 92: Northern view of the sixty-four Atlantes cubes.

The Clay Pavilion

Under the Beams

Álvaro Siza, Porto, Portugal

Bosco Sodi invited me to create a pavilion for the Casa Wabi Foundation, which fosters cultural exchange and artistic stimulation for children—a generation in search of improving their lives.

It is not possible to refuse a contribution, limited as it is, to such meaningful social work.

Sodi sent me pictures of the beautiful buildings by Tadao Ando, and I started working right away. I have to avoid long journeys, as much as that pains me, so architect Clemente Menéres went to Oaxaca and shared with me what he saw and felt.

Later, I had a meeting with Alfonso Quiñones, working on the project on behalf of Bosco Sodi, to whom I showed the first sketches: the pavilion, a storehouse, washing spaces, and an oven to be remade—all in the enclosed space of a round brick wall.

I asked him about materials and building techniques and about the experience of working on the first pavilions. When the drawing stage was finished, I kept in touch with Quiñones during construction.

I have just received photographs of the inhabited pavilion. Under the wood beams and the thatched roof, around a large table, a group of children sculpt with clay. Glances and smiles are exchanged; an atmosphere of hope can be felt. A whirlwind of a New World. I'm glad I answered the call.

The Orchid Pavilion

Ikigai at Casa Wabi

Bernardo Quinzaños, Centro de Colaboración Arquitectónica

The Orchid Pavilion is a wooden structure, permanent, sustainable, and lightweight, dedicated to the conservation of orchids in the Oaxaca region, which highlights the strong relationship between the biological and cultural diversity of the landscape.

As we approached the design of the Orchid Pavilion, our research pointed toward some clear technical features, components, and facts. It became evident that in order to grow, reproduce, and collect orchids, we needed to create the right environment for them to thrive: humid, partially shaded, and well-ventilated.

We were also interested in the relationship between the Japanese philosophy of *wabi-sabi*, which believes that beauty and harmony are found in simplicity, imperfection, and unconventionality, and the rich and complex traditions of the Oaxacan coast—its vernacular, locally sourced materials, and the high quality of the artisanal works of the local craftsmen. Then, unexpectedly, we thought of the Japanese word *ikigai*.

When somebody finds their purpose, their *ikigai*, they are more likely to lead a long, healthy life. However, it's easy to get lost in the stress and noise of our daily routine, so we need to make space, we need to chill out, in this case, with the orchids.

Our pavilion focuses on three main elements:

Firstly, the pavilion is a simple and austere machine. Twelve clay-based humidifiers utilize gravity to create a humid environment within the structure that houses orchids from the Oaxacan coast.

Secondly, the pavilion employs simple construction materials and techniques, including locally sourced wood and custom-made clay ceramic pieces baked in high-temperature kilns.

And thirdly, the pavilion serves as a sanctuary for the orchids while also aiming to evoke a profound sense of *ikigai* in its visitors.

The main element that allows orchids to thrive is a humid environment. The intricate roots, branches, and leaflets gather water from the air, soil, and all surfaces. A series of pyramid-shaped, water-filled clay basins rests at the top of a simple wooden structure. The basins slowly filter tiny droplets of water that fall to the ground, allowing for drip irrigation. The water is collected by clay-based trays that remain permanently humid. The breeze and heat enable the orchids to drink water directly from the environment, eliminating the need for manual watering of the specimens.

P. 101: A cool, semi-submerged space changes the horizon of visitors.
P. 102: After a long walk, a refuge to sit and drink water.
P. 103: The sound of dripping water resonates in the pavilion.
P. 104: Shade and calm to appreciate the diversity of orchid species.

The Chicken Pavilion

A Coop for Casa Wabi

Kengo Kuma, Kengo Kuma and Associates, Kanagawa, Japan

We were indeed surprised to receive such a rare commission. The unusual and exciting context of Casa Wabi allowed us to look at the proposal in a different light, and we saw an opportunity. Our studio usually takes on projects that will be inhabited by people and used for very specific purposes, though we are also well known for our challenging pavilion projects that generally don't have a precise function beyond experimentation itself. For Casa Wabi, we had the chance to combine the two approaches in the development of a pavilion with a specific function for its inhabitants, who happen to be chickens!

We conceived of this coop in a way that would relate to collective housing projects. While the sheltered space within this pavilion would be used for the general activities of the coop, the structure itself—built up by interlocking wooden boards—would create individual cells to be occupied by each of its inhabitants during their nightly roost. In addition, the permeable nature of our interlocking system lent itself well to an aired and shaded house.

With this interlocking system of 30-millimeter boards, we created lattice walls and a roof that would be able to withstand the main loads. For the horizontal loads, we tried to avoid the usual structural bracing by inserting rigid elements within each of the lattice cells. These rigid elements would locally limit the deformation of the lattice and therefore provide the overall bracing for the structure. Indeed, it's a pixelated kind of bracing.

In Japanese, the term *wabi* expresses an aesthetic that is essentially antagonistic to flashy colors and forms. A representative image of *wabi*, for example, would be an old, small farmhouse in late fall. In order to re-create this neutral and ascetic world on a faraway seaside of Mexico, we charred the wooden boards in a traditional method widely practiced in the western part of Japan. It not only helps the wood endure, but also gives a certain expression of serenity to a new construction, as if it had been there for over a century. Villages composed of such charred woods have a unique and exquisite atmosphere. We wanted to give the same kind of calmness to this collective housing for chickens.

P. 105: Casa Wabi chickens feed the foundation and the community.
P. 106: Kengo Kuma's sketch for the site.
Pp. 106–7: Partially completed charred-wood construction at dawn.
P. 108: Lattice structure allows chickens to enjoy shade and air.

Kalach Tower

Clay Kiln as Landmark

Alberto Kalach, Taller de Arquitectura X, Mexico City, Mexico

The 72-foot-tall brick Chacuaco, or chimney, was designed and built to hold the ceramic oven as a complementary piece to Casa Wabi's ceramic pavilion. Its conic shape tries to match and be part of the elegant curved brick wall of the clay workshop designed by Álvaro Siza.

The chimney is an homage to Aldo Rossi and Giorgio de Chirico; it is a symbol of fire and a distant landmark for the visitors of this unique natural reserve, with paths extending through 64 acres.

Following its structural logic, the thickness of the wall diminishes as it goes up. The brick pattern changes from more vibrant at the bottom, studded with triangular pieces, to smoother at the top. The chimney's shape echoes the thousands of cereus cacti that live in the surroundings, while its exaggerated height makes it distinctly the tallest structure in the flat landscape.

P. 109: Ground access to the kiln, used by local children to fire clay.
Pp. 110–11: Winding paths through the cacti and shrub surroundings.
P. 112: Triangular clay pieces add texture and redirect rain.

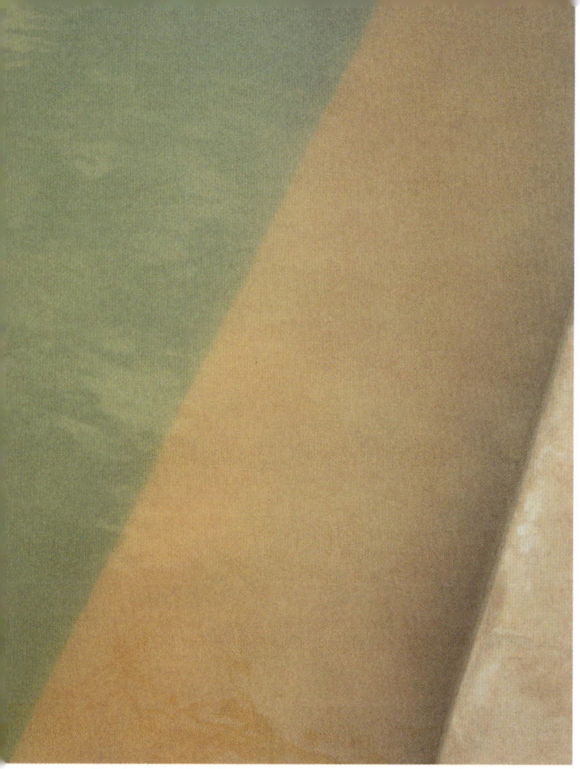

The Composting Pavilion

Descended from Another Sun

Gloria Cabral and Solano Benítez, Gabinete de Arquitectura, Mexico

Gabinete de Arquitectura was commissioned to build a composting pavilion for Casa Wabi. Constructed of humble materials, including recycled brick shards and cement, the tessellated walls create a pattern of light and shade. The pavilion serves not just Casa Wabi, but the communities that surround it, offering classes in composting as a cheap and ecologically friendly way to rejuvenate the soil. The architects of the pavilion describe it here.

To the architect it is not light that matters, it is the shadows.

The shadows—*las sombras, las umbras*—he seeds these from his beginnings; he deposits them in the doorway, sets them in the gates from his umbraculum (the papal canopy and symbol of his domain), where he announces the penumbra, the darkness that protects us all.

We build; we scatter some stones in the sky with the same insistence that fueled the Big Bang (which repeats endlessly). Some will believe, to their discredit, in their nonexistence, others that chance pinpoints their destiny. Still others will wonder if they are a religious fetish—stars as instruments of virtuous ordering—and they will name what we have done here with this building an act of anticipated resistance. The star thrower, however, will cultivate in this pavilion the essence of the shadows (infinite above all things), a few pendants in repetitive ceremony with each sunrise, which will help fertilize the earth for another season.

P. 121: Overview of the pavilion with noon shadows.
P. 122: Corner supports made of concrete injected with metal fibers.
P. 123, L: View toward concrete nooks for composting.
P. 123, R: Concept sketch for curtain walls of brick shards.
P. 124: Detail of recycled brick panels suspended with flexible cables.

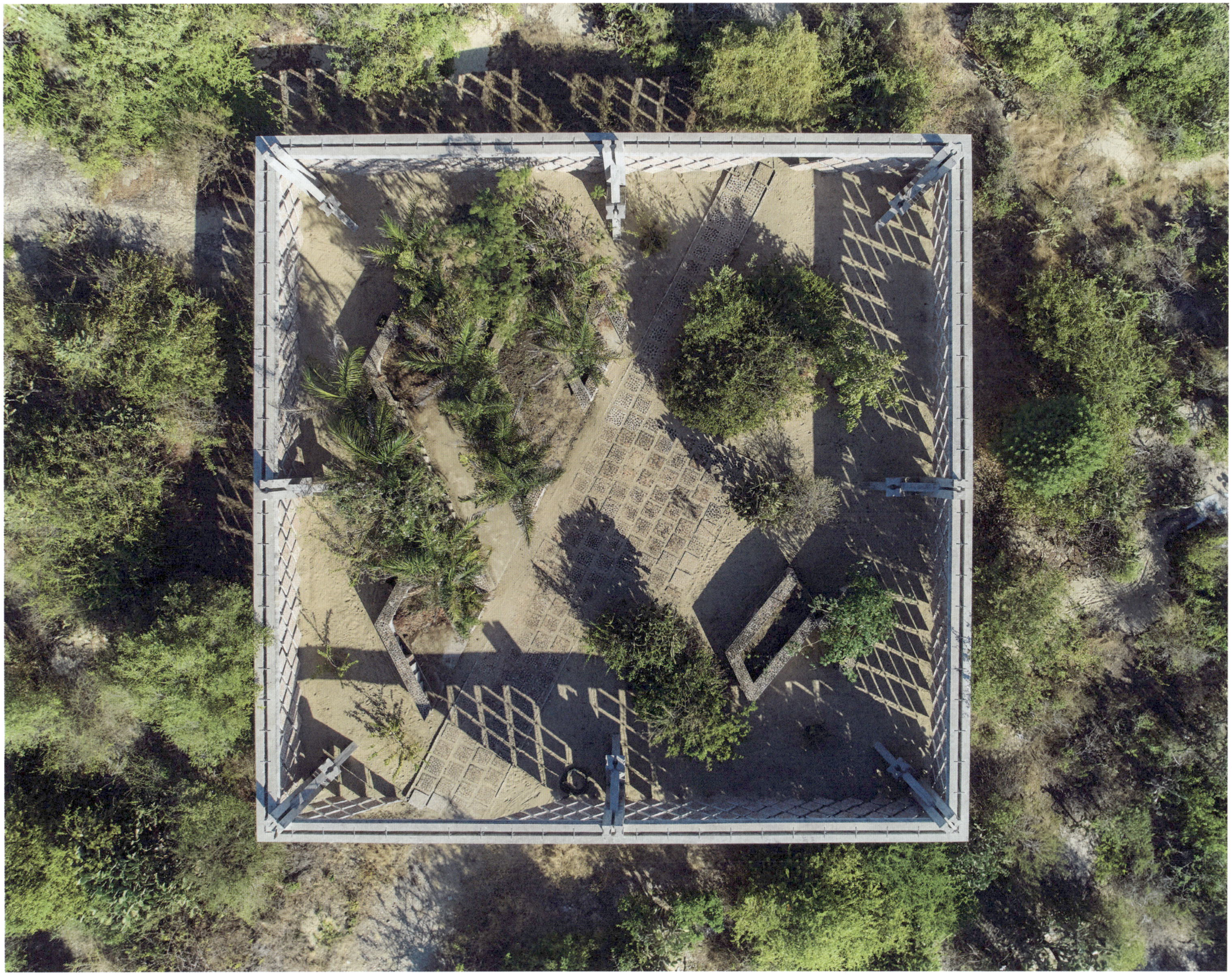

...el sembrador de estrellas

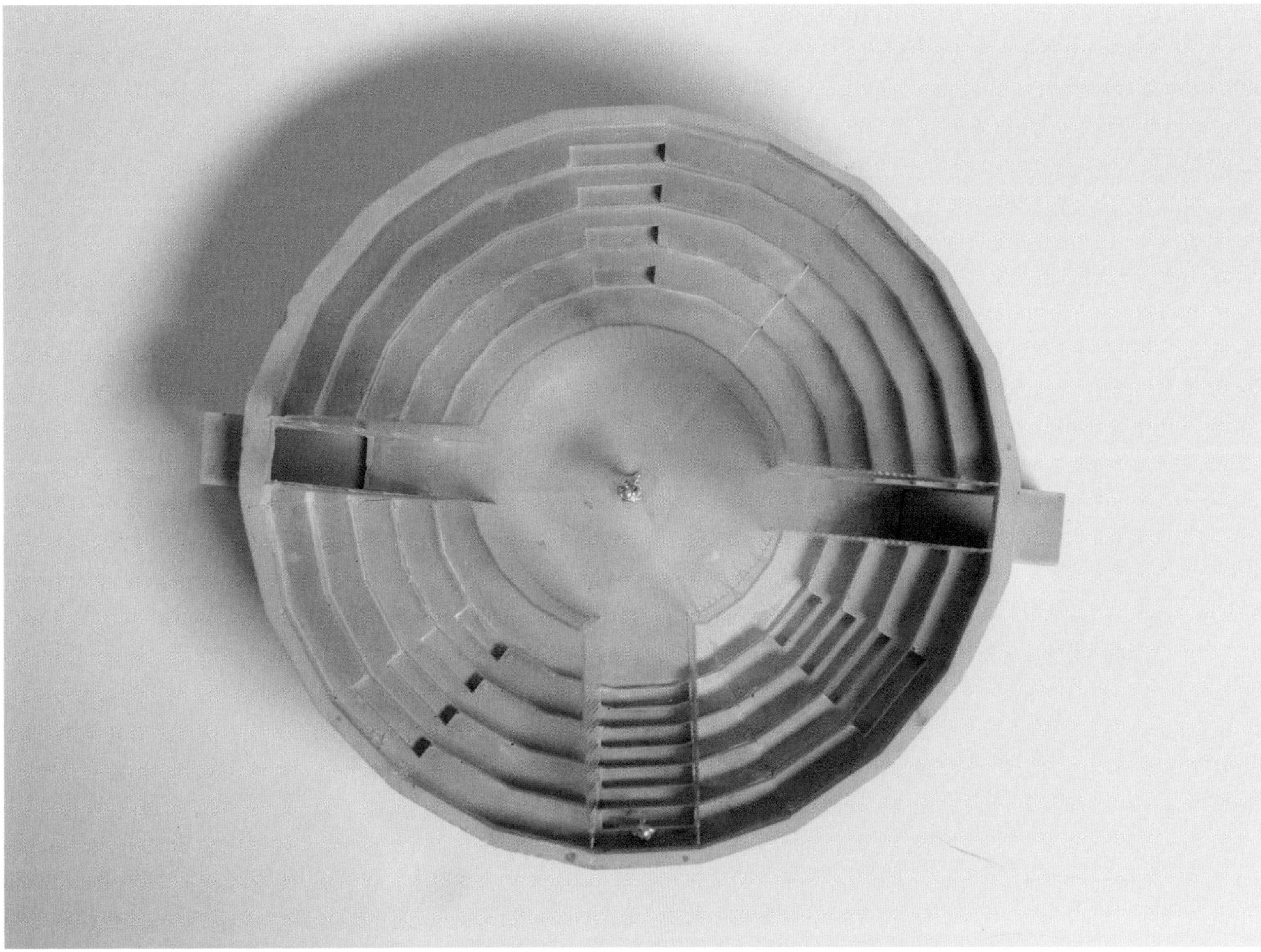

Sculpture Garden

A Work of Social Sculpture

Dakin Hart, Curator, Casa Wabi Foundation

Fundación Casa Wabi has several art collections: a growing array of architectural pavilions in the garden in Puerto Escondido dedicated to various domestic necessities and local environmental initiatives; works left by artists in the residency program as traces of their experience; and the site-specific sculptural installations documented here. At Casa Wabi these works are extremities that extend the capabilities of the body, not property.

The pavilions and installations were always part of the plan. In 2015, having only just completed construction, founder Bosco Sodi was already looking at how to extend Casa Wabi's reach—wanting it to spread roots and canopy along spatial, conceptual, and social axes. At that early moment, the next thing on his agenda was convincing the American sculptor Dan Graham (1942–2022) to build one of his glass-and-steel, art-as-a-mirror-of-society pavilions in the garden. Sodi was also imagining what he might do himself. One concept was to sink a shaft of water in the garden, deep enough for a determined swimmer to reach complete darkness. Replacing stultifyingly heat with bone-chilling cold, a trillion watts of excoriating sunlight with an equally crystalline darkness, the joint expanses of the Oaxacan coast and the Pacific Ocean, and all of their attendant noise, with the quiet claustrophobic embrace of a watery grave.

The Graham pavilion never materialized, and Sodi hasn't built the pool, which proved technically challenging in sand at sea level. But for two experiential works that aren't in the collection, they say a lot about the experimental environment Casa Wabi is meant to be and about how it uses the socializing power of aesthetic experience. The works that have subsequently been incorporated were created by artists who felt compelled to contribute something of themselves to what is a device of community. The collection has mostly developed around simple culturally resonant forms such as walls and totems. The walls mostly undermine the conventional divisiveness of walls, while the totems do what totems do: convey and mark civilizational intent. But the works that probably best explain how art augments Casa Wabi's social purpose are the juxtaposition of Sodi's *Atlantes* and the failed solid, six-foot cube half buried in the sand nearby. Together they suggest that over the course of time, the scale of human ambition and hubris is dwarfed and subsumed by our rise from, and return to, earth.

But the most important thing in the collection is not an object but a conviction: that integrating our consciousness with the world around us is essential to our well-being, and that this can be achieved by spending time together in a generative environment. To find these installations one traverses uncertain paths, under an excoriating sun, through an aggressive tangle of coastal desert in which nearly every living thing has spikes, spines, thorns, brambles, or sharp teeth of some kind. The works do not sport these same defenses because it is their job to lower ours.

P. 129: Side view of Bosco Sodi's Muro, *constructed of marble bricks.*
Pp. 130–31: Views of Uma Boa Ordem, *Héctor Zamora & Lucía Koch.*
P. 132: Huma Bhaba's cactus-like Sentinel, *made from Oaxacan clay.*
P. 133: Izumi Kato's distinctive figures on Bosco Sodi's clay sculpture.
Pp. 134–35: Op Art–inspired red soil Muro *by Claudia Comte.*
P. 136: Waterfall, *a plant-covered monolith by Bosco Sodi.*

Community Programs

To Your Roots to Go Forward

Rebeca Murrieta Valladares, Former Director Community Programs, Casa Wabi

Natural beauty, art, and millenary traditions merge magically in the state of Oaxaca, providing a vivid environment of cultural richness to those who visit it. Oaxaca is becoming a touchstone of Mexico to the world in part because its pre-Columbian and colonial arts are present in its cities, towns, markets, and artisan workshops—not just museums. Those traditions live through the people of Oaxaca, who have realized that their most important resource is their own cultural inheritance. Today, ancient cultures' artistic expressions and relationship with nature stay alive through colorful textiles made with natural dyes and fibers, black clay pottery, dry palm woven furniture, and exquisite cuisine. The reinstitution of local resources aesthetically and functionally has been a starting point for Casa Wabi's public programs, implemented in twelve communities that, due to their socioeconomic status, have shifted away from their cultural identity and tradition. Staff at Casa Wabi work with communities in a manner of deep respect and a firm conviction that we are the ones who can learn the most from them. Invited artists lead experiences exploring tastes, colors, and contact with nature, while local inhabitants reinterpret their environment, recover their roots, and access different types of cultural products that complement their formal education. Casa Wabi generates exchange between international contemporary culture and these twelve communities through five essential avenues: a residency, exhibitions, recovery of the local clay (public classes), a film program, and a mobile library.

In the clay program, we conduct workshops for schoolchildren, encouraging interaction between children and clay in order to give value back to the use of this primal material. Since there are no cinemas or theaters in the area, we brought Mexican film productions to communities through outdoor screenings and a cinema matinee program for children in Casa Wabi's auditorium. The space is also used as a venue for local film festivals. Casa Wabi created an alliance with one of the most important foundations of Oaxaca, Fundación Alfredo Harp Helú, to implement a mobile library that services the coast. The van-library transports a collection of more than six hundred books for the public, visiting schools and parks to promote reading and book culture.

P. 137: Children from a local school visit Casa Wabi.
Pp. 138–39: Community art interventions in Tiltepec, Oaxaca.
P. 140: Buckets for sale and clay tablets curing, Tiltepec.
P. 141: Sculptural interventions on buildings and parks in Oaxaca.
P. 142, T: Air drying sea salt in El Venado.
P. 142, B: A community project with clay in Agua Zarca.
P. 143: Elements of wabi-sabi and clay-making in El Zapotalito.
P. 144: Partial walls creating shade and places to play.

AV 16 SEPTIEMBRE
CENTRO.

Building Casa Wabi

Six Years in the Sun

Alfonso Quiñones, BAAQ', Mexico City, Mexico

As the architect invited to work on behalf of Casa Wabi, I witnessed the project develop in stages over six years, including two phases of collaboration. The first phase began with Tadao Ando. We met in Osaka to present him with my team's proposals for Casa Wabi's palapas, as well as the preliminary construction drawings we had created over the previous four months. Later we visited Álvaro Siza to finalize the details of his clay pavilion. He wanted to know every detail about the children who were going to use the space: their culture, their customs, even their meal times. The next two collaborations with Kengo Kuma and Solano Benítez gave my team the opportunity to learn their processes of design, values, and philosophies, an experience that I treasure deeply.

The second phase of collaboration—as critical and impactful as the first—happened on the ground during construction, working with the community. From the first day, the local workers took on the project as their own. Their techniques and talent permeated every element, and Casa Wabi inherited their culture and essence. After a long planning process, and considering the location and access to technology of the site, we realized the best way to carry out the construction was by hand. This meant that the concrete, the carpentry, and each brick would be made at Casa Wabi by local craftsmen. The castings were made in batches with small buckets and mixers, a process that began as soon as the first ray of sunlight emerged. Each worker had a specific task: carry material, throw the mixture, or monitor the proportions in each station, for example. Each day after casting, at lunchtime, we celebrated—but always with some anticipation and uncertainty, since we wouldn't know if the casting had set successfully until the next day. In the afternoon, the forms had to be moved with the greatest precision, prepared in order to comply with the geometric rigor of Tadao Ando's design. After a few attempts at casting using a sophisticated but inefficient process, a local master builder came up with an idea for several workers to raise the levers on the shoring at the same time; the resulting scene was reminiscent of rowers moving an ancient boat's oars. That's just one of many examples in which the workers' ingenuity allowed us to optimize both the speed and quality of the work.

Casa Wabi is an encounter between art and community that takes place through architecture, and we had the honor to witness this through shared work and humanity. I thank each of the workers, bricklayers, *palaperos*, carpenters, teachers of trade, my office, external consultants, my partner in this project, Joaquin Castillo, the resident architects, and especially Bosco Sodi for inviting me to participate in this great life experience.

P. 145: Wooden frame, and weaving process, for palapa roof.
Pp. 146–47: Mock-ups to test concrete curing methods.
P. 147, T: Detail of oculus in mock-up structure.
P. 148: Teams hoisting royal palms for Bosco Sodi's studio roof.
P. 149: Details with and without wooden bracing from casting.
Pp. 150–51: Details of worker constructing Kengo Kuma's lattice.
P. 152, T: Casa Wabi vegetation ten years after construction.
P. 152, B: Southern panorama of construction and full wall.

Afterword

On the Ground in Oaxaca

Alex Iida, Architect, Tadao Ando Architect & Associates

My first visit to Puerto Escondido, Mexico, was in 2011. From the airport, visitors drive down through the mountain; I visually captured the entire project site with a vast ocean backdrop and no other structure on the nearly two miles of shoreline.

An imaginary horizontal line, parallel with the coastline, appeared on the site from a distance, and seemed to ask for an elegant addition to the local landscape. The main approach is in the middle of a 341-yard-long concrete wall followed by a 54-yard pool on the ocean side, naturally forming four zones.

Along both sides of the wall is the main pathway connecting all programs via subtle openings in the wall. The openings frame the beach and the sea on the south, and the vast green and mountains on the north, all wrapped under the open sky.

A singular long wall directs visitors to wander throughout the site. Time of nothingness accompanied only by the sound of waves and breeze, and the light reflecting off the wall changing throughout the day, seems to provide meditative energy to purify, reflect, and be inspired.

A traditional roof system, palapa, by local artisans was most appropriate. To achieve the foundation's goal of cultural exchange through art, respect, and integrating the local culture was crucial. Palapa was lifted slightly up from geometric concrete beams and walls to let it breathe, and to create a portal to let in gentle light.

During construction, we used horses to go around the site, and once saw a large crocodile swimming in the pool.

The concrete cylinder was planned as a meditative space at the eastern end of the site. However, due to construction constraints the arc was deformed with layers of textured surface. This unintentional occurrence inspired the logo for Casa Wabi, following the definition of the Japanese term *wabi-sabi*, finding beauty in imperfection.

Although there was a language barrier, the energy, willingness, and pride I felt from all the locals I encountered throughout the project were inspiring. This was the driving force that led to the success of the foundation and the continuing architectural additions on site to date.

Understanding the local environment, feeling the site, dialogue, and collaboration with all parties involved, is the key to giving life and lasting success to this project.

Pp. 154–55: Southeastern cactus garden next to residency housing.

Casa Wabi

Bosco Sodi and Lucía Corredor
Founders

Carla Sodi
General Director

Dakin Hart
Curator

Gustavo Gutiérrez
Resource Administration

Juan Pino
Community Development and Residence Director

Gustavo Parra
Director of Community Programs

Mariana Vinalay
Artist Liaison

Dulce López
Clay Pavilion Coordinator

Manuel Magaña
Mobile Library Coordinator

Armando Zenteno Bucio
Tour Guide

Rafael A. Balboa
Casa NaNo's Director

Kitchen Staff
Emilia Matus Ruiz, Rosibel Carmona Torres, Patricia Yareli Quintas, Perla Anahí Naranjo, Zaira Jazmín Cortés, Sandra Vázquez

Gardening Team
José Arias Triste, Edgar Rubén Carmona Torres, José Luis Arias Matus, Alberto Vázquez, Bernardo Salinas

Visiting Casa Wabi

Casa Wabi Puerto Escondido, Oaxaca
Carretera Federal Salina Cruz
Santiago Pinotepa Nacional Km. 113
Puerto Escondido, Oaxaca 71983

Guided tours available
Mandatory reservation
Tour schedule
Monday to Friday
10:00 am, 12:00 pm, 4:00 pm
Saturday and Sunday
10:00 am, 12:00 pm, 2:00 pm

Casa Wabi Offices and Gallery, Mexico City
Sabino 336, Atlampa, Cuauhtémoc
Mexico City 06450
Exhibition schedule
Tuesday through Sunday: 10 am to 5 pm

Casa Wabi is a nonprofit organization that relies on private and public funding. These funds are used to fully finance the foundation's activities in Oaxaca.

If you would like to donate, please contact donate@casawabi.org or reach us through www.casawabi.org.

Architects' Biographies

Tadao Ando
Tadao Ando's work in reinforced concrete has won him international recognition, beginning with the Pritzker Architecture Prize in 1995. His structures—from homes to museums to places of worship or public use—define spaces in new ways that allow for constantly changing patterns of light and wind. His concrete is often referred to as "smooth-as-silk" and exists as both structure and surface. The evenly spaced holes that remain from the casting process have become an Ando signature, as has his knowledge of wood and the carpenter's craft. As a child, he closely observed woodworking shops, and how trees grew and changed under the sun's shifting light, which in turn changed the qualities of the trees' lumber. He came to understand the absolute balance between a form and the material from which it is made.

Ambrosi Etchegaray
Jorge Ambrosi and Gabriela Etchegaray established the Ambrosi Etchegaray art and architecture studio in Mexico City in 2011. They curated Mexico's pavilion at the 2018 Venice International Architecture Biennale. The pair teach at Columbia University's Graduate School of Architecture, Planning and Preservation and have served as critics and lecturers at national and international architecture schools. *Architectural Record* selected them for Design Vanguard 2017 and Emerging Voices 2015.

Solano Benítez
Born in Asunción, Paraguay, Solano Benítez graduated from the School of Architecture at the National University of Asunción (FAUNA). In 1987, he founded Gabinete de Arquitectura, which he shares with Alberto Marinoni and Gloria Cabral. He has received many prizes, including the Junior Chamber of Paraguay's Outstanding Youth Award for his contributions to national culture (1999), the BSI Swiss Architectural Award (2008), and Honorable Mention in Paraguay's National Congress for contributions to the country (2011). Also in 2011, the Paraguay Architects Association named him Architect of the Bicentenary, and in 2012 he became an Honorary Fellow of the American Institute of Architects.

Alberto Kalach
Born and raised in Mexico City, Alberto Kalach studied architecture at the Universidad Iberoamericana in Mexico City and at Cornell University in Ithaca, New York. He has made numerous projects that range from low-income urban housing to the hydrological rescue plan for the Mexico Basin's entire valley.

Kengo Kuma
Kengo Kuma is one of Japan's leading contemporary architects. His work expresses the emotional content of materials and connects with their intrinsic characteristics in construction, as well as with the teachings of Japanese tradition. Kuma graduated from Tokyo University in 1979 and opened the Spatial Design Studio in 1987. In 1990, he opened Kengo Kuma & Associates in Tokyo and then a Paris office in 2008. He teaches at Tokyo University's Graduate School of Architecture and has received prestigious international awards, including Finland's Spirit of Nature Wood Architecture Award, the Grand Prize for JCD Design Award, the prize for Cultural Public Institutions for Kiro-san Observatory in Ehime, and the Minister of Education, Culture, Sports, Science, and Technology's Art Encouragement Prize.

Álvaro Siza
Portuguese architect Álvaro Siza graduated from the University of Porto School of Architecture, and in 1954 opened a practice in Porto. He teaches architecture at the University of Porto and has been a visiting professor at Harvard University, the University of Pennsylvania, Los Andes University of Bogotá, and Lausanne's École polytechnique fédérale. He has received numerous honors and awards, including the Alvar Aalto Medal, the Mies van der Rohe Foundation Award, and Harvard University's first Veronica Rudge Green Prize.

OMA/Shohei Shigematsu
Established in 2001, OMA New York is responsible for the studio's operations in the Americas and Japan. Shohei Shigematsu is a Partner at OMA who has been leading a diverse portfolio of projects with an interdisciplinary approach to design. Shigematsu has overseen the completion of cultural projects from museums to exhibitions, including Milstein Hall at Cornell University (2011), Faena Forum (2016), extension to Quebec National Museum (2016), Tiffany & Co. Landmark (2023), and the Buffalo AKG Art Museum (2023). He has collaborated with fashion brands such as Prada, Dior, and Louis Vuitton, as well as artists including Cai Guo-Qiang, Marina Abramovic, and Taryn Simon. He is currently overseeing the construction of the New Museum, OMA's first public cultural building in New York.

Centro de Colaboración Arquitectónica (CCA)
The studio operates as an independent platform dedicated to researching, conceptualizing, and developing architectural and urban projects focused on making a positive impact on their immediate surroundings and on society more broadly. As an interdisciplinary practice, CCA has been able to capitalize on the knowledge, talent, and creativity of each of its team members to generate ideas through an inclusive and collaborative working method. Founder Bernardo Quinzaños began his career in the visual arts and has participated in numerous architecture and art exhibitions both in Mexico and abroad.

Architecture Teams

Tadao Ando Architect & Associates
Tadao Ando: Lead architect
Alex Ida: Architect in charge and project manager
Alfonso Quiñones: Architect and project manager in Mexico

Ambrosi Etchegaray
Jorge Ambrosi and Gabriela Etchegaray: Lead architects
Ivo Martins and Santiago Bonilla: Architects in charge
Javier Caro: Collaborator

Gabinete de Arquitectura
Solano Benítez: Lead architect and architect in charge
Alfonso Quiñones and Alfonso Sodi: Architects and project managers in Mexico

Taller de Arquitectura X
Alberto Kalach: Lead architect

Kengo Kuma and Associates
Kengo Kuma: Lead architect
Javier Villa: Architect in charge and project manager
Alfonso Quiñones: Architect and project manager in Mexico

Álvaro Siza
Álvaro Siza: Lead architect
Clemente Menéres: Architect in charge and project manager
Alfonso Quiñones: Architect and project manager in Mexico

OMA New York
Shohei Shigematsu: Partner-in-Charge
Shary Tawil, Caroline Corbett: Project Architect
Francesco Rosati, Dylan Wei, Patricio Fernandez, Yiyao Wang, Alireza Shojakhani, Cameron Fullmer: Team

Centro de Colaboración Arquitectónica (CCA)
Bernardo Quinzaños: Architect
Begoña Manzano, Andrés Suárez, Miguel Izaguirre, Florencio de Diego, Carlos Cruz Ay, Javier Castillo, Carlos Molina, Fernanda Ventura: Team

Acknowledgments

The Casa Wabi Foundation would like to thank Bosco Sodi for his vision and commitment to the development of culture in our country. A great thank-you is due to Lucía Corredor, a pillar to the foundation. We would like to thank Tadao Ando, Alberto Kalach, Álvaro Siza, Kengo Kuma, Gabriela Etchegaray, Jorge Ambrosi, Solano Benítez, Gloria Cabral, Bernardo Quinzaños, and Shohei Shigematsu for translating their ideas into reality. Across all projects, we would like to thank Alex Iida and our architects and project managers in Mexico, Alfonso Quiñones, Samantha Redfern, and Patricio Sodi. Additionally, we would like to acknowledge the maestro José Ramírez, for his infallible work during the construction of all buildings in Casa Wabi. Thanks to Daniel Buren, Michel François, Harold Ancart, Jannis Kounellis, Ugo Rondinone, Izumi Kato, Huma Bhabha, Claudia Comte, José Dávila, and Richard Long for sharing their creativity through their exhibitions and interventions. Thanks to all residents for their contributions to the development of the region. Thanks to all the members of the communities who welcome us into their way of living.

To our sponsors, who have believed in our mission and have helped us build this project since the beginning: Punta Pájaros, DECADA, Casa Cuervo, Fundación Alfredo Harp Helú, Mantarraya Producciones, Grupo Habita, Cementos Fortaleza, Hotel Escondido, IMCINE, TEKA, and Giorno Poetry Systems, among many others, thank you. Thanks to all our donors who have joined us in this project; with their support, we have been able to reach higher and higher.

We are always grateful to Luis Urrutia, María García Sainz Creel, Garry Hattem, Tatiana Bilbao, Eugenia Braniff, and Pablo León de la Barra for sharing their expertise, leadership, and generosity, as well as to Shari Tawil and Clemente Menéres. We thank our supporters Pablo Velasco, Jaime Romandía, Francisco del Valle, Emily Santangelo, José Juan Rivera Ríos, Demetrio Sodi, Mauricio Galguera, Alfonso Molina, Claudio Sodi Zapata, Jaime Corredor Esnaola, Jaime Isita Portilla, Alejandra Sánchez Aldana, Eduardo Sánchez Navarro, Jorge Muriel, Ignacio Muñoz, Loti Ambrosi, Carmina Mogollon, Tomás Urrutia, Serapión Fernández, Francisco Fernández, Lupe Philips, Leonor Isita, Ana Francisca Velasco Sodi, Carlos Zedillo, and Kazu Yoshii. Thanks to every visitor and ally who has contributed to this project.

We are most appreciative of our General Director Carla Sodi Ambrosi for leading this great team. Thanks to Dakin Hart, Gustavo Gutiérrez, Juan Pino, Gustavo Parra, Rafael Balboa, Mariana Vinalay, Dulce López, Manuel Magaña, Armando Zenteno, Diego Arellanes, and to our amazing staff, Chepe, Emi, Rosi, Perla, Paty, Edgar, Alberto, Astrid, and Sandra. Thanks to Alberto Ríos de la Rosa, Genaro Guevara, Rebeca Murrieta Valladares, Paola Herrera, Maribel Zorrilla, Brian Reséndiz, and everyone who is and has been a member of our team, for their commitment and for their everyday efforts to build a better society through their labor and dedication.

First published in the United States in 2024 by

Rizzoli Electa
A Division of Rizzoli International Publications, Inc.
300 Park Avenue South
New York, NY 10010
www.rizzoliusa.com

Copyright © 2024 Fundación Casa Wabi AC

All rights reserved. No part of this publication may be reproduced, stored in a retrieval system, or transmitted in any form or by any means, electronic, mechanical, photocopying, recording, or otherwise, without prior consent of the publishers.

This is a revised edition of a book with the same title originally published in 2018.

Library of Congress Control Number: 2018958062

ISBN-13: 978-0-8478-4783-9

For Rizzoli Electa:
Publisher: Charles Miers
Associate Publisher: Margaret Rennolds Chace
Editor: Loren Olson
Copyeditors: Gail Spilsbury and Elizabeth Smith
Proofreader: Richard Slovak
Production Manager: Maria Pia Gramaglia

Designed by SARCO

2024 2025 2026 2027 / 10 9 8 7 6 5 4 3 2 1

Printed and bound in Italy

MIX
Paper | Supporting responsible forestry
FSC® C013123

Photo Credits:
Eduardo Amaro: Pp. 93, 95, 96, 97 (bottom); Alfonso López Baz: Pp. 34–35, 53 (bottom left), 78, 80; Diego Berruecos: Pp. 67–69, 132; Samuel Boutruche: Pp. 26 (bottom), 74 (right), 98 (right); Estudio Michel Zabé: cover; Pp. 10–11, 14, 29, 32 (left), 46 (bottom), 49, 50, 52, 53 (top and bottom left), 54 (top), 62–63, 148, 154–55; Estudio Solano Benítez: P. 123 (right); Sofía Fernández: Pp. 86, 87, 88, 140 (both), 142 (bottom), 143; Michel François: P. 59 (right); Rafael Gamo: Pp. 102, 104; Sofía Gonzalez Noriega: Pp. 13, 15 (top), 16, 28, 32 (right), 36 (left), 37 (right), 41 (both), 42, 44–45, 54 (bottom), 55 (bottom), 56, 58–59, 73; Jean Sebástien Gregoire: P. 61; Arlette del Hoyo: Pp. 89, 110–12; Kengo Kuma Associates: P. 106 (left); Sergio López: Pp. 17 (left), 18–21, 25, 26 (top), 33, 36–37 (middle), 40, 48, 51, 57, 60 (all), 70–71, 74 (left), 75–77, 79–80, 82–85, 89–92, 97 (top), 98 (left), 99 (both), 105, 106–9, 113, 114–15, 116 (both), 117–24, 129–31, 133, 136, 138 (top), 139, 141, 150–51, 152 (top), Endpapers; Jaime Navarro: Pp. 101, 103; Gustavo Eduardo Nigenda Vasquez: 134–35; OMA: Pp. 125–128; Gustavo Parra: Pp. 55, 138 (bottom), 147 (both); Ana Pichardo: P. 142 (top); Santiago de la Puente: P. 66; Ilán Rabchinskey: Pp. 30–31; Diego Rivero: P. 144; Fernanda Romandia: Pp. 100, 145 (top), 146 (all), 149 (both), 152 (bottom); Yusuke Sato: P. 64; Carla Sodi Ambrosi: P. 145 (bottom); Maria Sprowls: P. 65; Edmund Sumer: Pp. 15 (bottom), 27, 38, 39, 43, 72; Michael Toolan: Pp. 12, 17 (right), 46 (top), 47, 94 (both), 137

Martino Stierli Notes:
1. Tadao Ando, “Wall: The Time‘s Building, 1984: On the Takasegawa River, Kyoto, Japan,” *Perspecta 25* (1989): 211.
2. Tadao Ando, “From Self-Enclosed Modern Architecture towards Universality” (1982), quoted in Fredric Jameson, “Tadao Ando and the Enclosure of Modernism,” *ANY: Architecture New York 6* (1994): 29.

The Residency Program

Three Dialogues for a Cultural Exchange

Carla Sodi Ambrosi, General Director, Casa Wabi Foundation

"Culture is mix. Culture means a mix of things from other sources."—Orhan Pamuk

The Casa Wabi Foundation's principal mission is based on the belief that a personal encounter with the arts is an instrument for social and cultural transformation. With this idea in mind, the residency program was created as a vehicle to facilitate exchanges between people involved in national and international arts and those living in communities of Oaxaca's coast. Since October 2014, the foundation has allocated its resources to the residency program through the fostering of three key dialogues.

The first dialogue relies on the creative process of each artist. The residency at Casa Wabi is a cosmos far removed from the whirlwind of the contemporary art world. It's a refuge where the artist can stop worrying about everyday affairs and find more time for an inner dialogue that eventually generates new ways of thinking. Thus, the interdisciplinary residencies offer participants a unique opportunity to focus exclusively on their work, while at the same time exploring, expanding, and developing their practice.

The second dialogue is based on the personal and professional exchange among residents. Theoretical and intellectual growth is facilitated through the interaction with other artists, writers, filmmakers, dancers, or other members of the cultural milieu the program provides. The foundation selects six residents per period based on the quality of their work and their potential to create meaningful projects and to engage in conversation with the other residents. This method allows the curatorial department to carefully construct residency periods where emerging artists work side by side with internationally acclaimed artists. We strive to gather a diverse group, including artists of different nationalities, backgrounds, and ages who often go on to pursue collective projects after the residency ends.

The third dialogue takes place between residents and members of the fourteen neighboring communities with which we work. The foundation capitalizes on the artists' creative and intellectual talents in innovative ways to benefit the surrounding villages. The interdisciplinary projects that develop take on many forms, as residents have total freedom to propose positive ideas to their community groups. This sensitive dialogue is successful when everyone shares knowledge, experiences, and different ways of thinking—it's a melting pot where varying worldviews come together in a constructive way.

Through the context of these dialogues, the foundation not only advocates artistic education for social development, but also offers a rewarding model.

P. 49: Southwest wall toward residency housing at sunset.
Pp. 50–51: Six private residency bungalows with beach paths.
P. 52: Austere residency housing with wooden bedframes.
P. 53: Paths between bungalows and studios in eastern wall.
Pp. 54–55: Interior and details from artists' studios and kitchen.
P. 56: Table outside communal studio with beachcomber's finds.

The Mushroom Pavilion

An Incubator of Cuisine and Community

OMA/Shohei Shigematsu, New York

The function of the Mushroom Pavilion, as its name suggests, is to cultivate fungi, but also the exchange between food and the local communities of Puerto Escondido by teaching them about the growth process. It will also be integrated into the kitchen of the foundation and of Hotel Escondido. To convey this simple yet important purpose, we conceived a pavilion as a basic, oval form. Like an incubating egg, the self-supporting ellipsoid is derived from an optimized interior organization for growing mushrooms.

Within, the domed interior is divided into three chambers—fruiting room, incubation room, and storage—encircling a gathering space at the heart of the pavilion. The lower half of the bowl is stepped, like an amphitheater in the round, to make shelves for handmade terra-cotta mushroom pots crafted by local artisans. The stepping and elliptical form create a panopticon viewing experience, rendering the mushroom growing process visible in its entirety.

An oculus opens up the central space to the sky and fills the cave-like interior with light, while additional openings around the lower perimeter enable natural ventilation. A platform and portal at the top of the steps offer views above and beyond the natural brush to the ocean. The three-dimensional volume curves inward at its base to minimize the pavilion's contact on the ground, preserving the natural landscape as much as possible and allowing the native guayacán to thrive. Its concrete shell is burlap stamped on the outside to retain the site's high-iron-content water. Conceding to the natural elements, the pavilion will rust and change in appearance over time.

P. 125: Detail of burlap-stamped concrete shell material.
P. 126: View of oculus, openings, and viewing portal.
P. 127: Overhead view of stepped shelves and gathering space.
P. 128: Side view of curved walls and domed roof.

The Guayacan Nursery

How to Touch a Tree

Damián Comas for Jorge Ambrosi and Gabriela Etchegaray

Place an ear to a tree trunk at night. What does it say? Do the same in the morning, then during the rainy season, and then in the months that follow, during the drought. How is it different? Isn't it obvious that everything changes, that we must all travel between heat and cold, water and thirst, presences and voids, life and death? The *wabi-sabi* architecture of the guayacan nursery was born from these principles and oppositions. An expression of matter and space itself, it was developed by architects Jorge Ambrosi and Gabriela Etchegaray, conceived as a nursery for trees that in its transition through space and time will benefit from its deterioration and its assimilation into the landscape, into nature, into the principle of all things. A minimum use of materials achieves the maximum expression. The purpose is to present and care for *Guaiacum sanctum* (Zygophyllaceae), an endemic and threatened species commonly known as guayacan.

In order to protect guayacan, Casa Wabi in collaboration with Oaxaca's Environmental Management Unit decided to create a nursery for the trees' care and reproduction. From inception, its authors understood that the architecture would be only a medium for the expressions that nature offers. The nursery's paths are below ground level, so visitors are invited to relate to the trees in a new way: to perceive the temperature, the humidity of the environment, the flow of the wind, the relationship between the species and the water of the subsoil.

Containing an imperfect and elegant beauty in its austerity, the nursery's entrance welcomes visitors with a shadow cast by a giant water table that functions as the threshold of access and, in turn, creates a living space for workers and visitors—where the sun, water, and wind become evident and invite observation of the guayacan in close proximity, to know and recognize it in an environment that expresses depth, emotion, intelligence, and mysticism. Then, visitors walk toward the crops of trees that rise up in a sequence of work tables, rising above a gradual excavation into the land. Throughout this irregular plan, care for the environment is evident, as is a respect for those who work it: it is much easier for workers to water, observe, and take care of the trees when they don't need to stoop down to ground level. The guayacan nursery is undoubtedly a contemporary architecture—one that is committed to an aesthetic, to the environment, to the passage of time, and to the care of our Mexican land.

P. 113: Overview of the guayacan nursery.
Pp. 114–15: Northern view of water table and access steps.
P. 116: Details of water table and flowering shrubs.
P. 117: View from shaded entrance area toward planters.
P. 118: Overview of western approach and service road.
P. 119: Guayacan planters are waist-high for easy access.
P. 120: Water table collects and directs rainwater to plants.